Let's Start! ART

Drawing

Sue Nicholson

QED Publishing

First published in the UK in 2005 by
QED Publishing
A Quarto Group company
226 City Road
London EC1V 2TT

www.qed-publishing.co.uk

A Catalogue record for this book is available from the British Library.

ISBN 1 84538 165 3

Written by Sue Nicholson
Designed by Susi Martin
Editor Paul Manning
Photographer Michael Wicks

Publisher Steve Evans
Creative Director Louise Morley
Editorial Manager Jean Coppendale

Printed and bound in China

The author and publisher would like to thank Billy and Dylan Sarah Morley for making the models.

Picture credits
Corbis /Caroline Penn 6, /Kevin Fleming 19, /Richard Cummings 22
Getty Images /Steve Bly/Stone 15, /Bridgeman Art Library 17
The Art Archive /Musée des Arts Africains et Océaniens /Dagli Orti 13
Travelsite /Neil Setchfield 9, 11
Werner Forman/British Museum /21

Note to teachers and parents

The projects in this book are aimed at children at Key Stage 1 and are presented in order of difficulty, from easy to more challenging. Each can be used as a stand-alone activity or as part of another area of study.

While the ideas in the book are offered as inspiration, children should always be encouraged to work from their own imagination and first-hand observations.

Sourcing ideas

★ Encourage the children to source ideas from their own experiences as well as from books, magazines, the Internet, galleries or museums.

★ Prompt them to talk about different types of art they have seen at home or on holiday.

★ Use the 'Click for Art!' boxes as a starting point for finding useful material on the Internet.*

★ Suggest that each child keeps a sketchbook of his or her ideas.

Evaluating work

★ Encourage the children to share their work and talk about their ideas and ways of working. What do they like best/least about it? If they did it again, what would they do differently?

★ Help the children to judge the originality of their work and to appreciate the different qualities in others' work. This will help them to value ways of working that are different from their own.

★ Encourage the children by displaying their work.

* Website information is correct at the time of going to press. However, the publishers cannot accept liability for information or links found on third-party websites.

Contents

Words in bold, **like this**, are explained in the Glossary on page 24.

Getting started

In this book, you'll learn how to make your drawings better. All you need are a few basic things.

Top tip
Always carry a **sketchbook** with you for quick on-the-spot drawings. You can turn them into finished pictures later.

Drawing pencils

Eraser

Drawing materials

Pencils come in different grades. Look for the numbers and letters on the side.

2H = Hard. Good for light, sharp lines and details

HB = Medium-hard. Good for sketching

2B = Soft. Good for wide, soft lines and shading

An eraser is used for rubbing out pencil lines.

Charcoal is good for quick, bold sketches.

Chalk comes in different colours. Use it for sketches or to colour in large areas.

Charcoal

Chalk

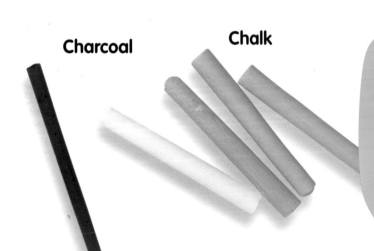

Top tip
Try using different materials and papers. A thick soft pencil, charcoal or chalk on rough paper gives an interesting **texture**.

Pastels

Coloured pencils

Felt-tip pens

Pastels can be oil or chalk. Oil pastels are brighter, but both types are soft and crumbly. You can smudge pastels to make blurred lines.

Felt-tip pens are useful for adding detail and strong black lines.

Wax crayons come in lots of different colours. They are good for bold, colourful pictures.

Wax crayons

Paper

You can draw on many types of paper. Smooth **cartridge paper** is best for pen and pencil drawings.

Rough **sugar paper** is good for charcoal, chalk, pastels and crayons.

Sugar paper

Cartridge paper

Safety tips

Sharpen pencils with a pencil sharpener. Use safety scissors when cutting paper or card.

Pencil work

Make your drawings more realistic and **three-dimensional** by adding **shading** and **highlights**.

Top tip
For an interesting texture, try shading with the side of a pencil or the wide edge of a stick of charcoal.

Shading and highlights

Shading is a way of making parts of a picture look darker.

You can rub out parts of your shading and make white shiny highlights with an eraser.

Smoky steam train

Look at this drawing of a steam train made with charcoal.

Charcoal smudged with a fingertip to make smoke

Front of train heavily shaded to look darker

Shading rubbed out with an eraser to make highlights

Short, spiky lines for grass

Click for Art!

To see a drawing by van Gogh, go to **www.ibiblio.org/wm/paint/auth/gogh/fields/** Scroll down and click on 'Wheat Field with Sun and Cloud'.

Practise different ways of adding texture to your drawings.

Scribbled lines look like wool

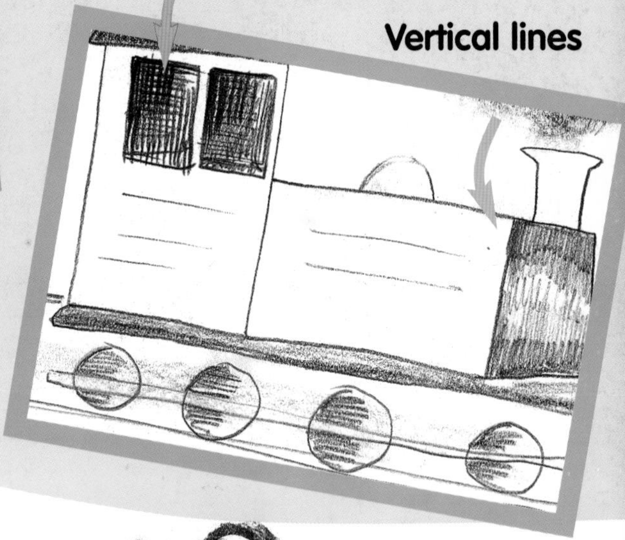

Criss-cross lines (cross-hatching)

Vertical lines

Angled lines look like grass

Short lines going in the same direction (hatching)

Self-portrait

A self-portrait is a picture of YOU, the artist. Making a self-portrait is a good way to learn how to draw faces.

I Using a soft pencil, lightly draw an egg shape for the outline of your face.

Using a mirror

Take a good look at your face in a large mirror. Try smiling, then frowning, then looking sad. Watch how your **features** change.

Click for Art!

To see a self-portrait by Peter Blake, go to **www.tate.org.uk/collection/** Search on 'Peter Blake', 'Self-portrait with Badges'. To see a self-portrait by Frida Kahlo, go to **www.artchive.com/artchive/K/kahlo/kahlo_trotsky.jpg.html**

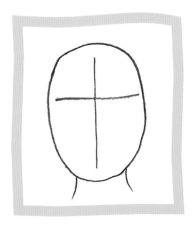 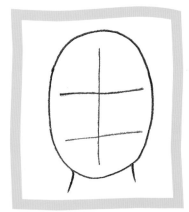 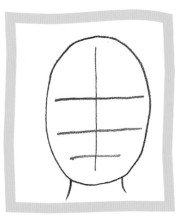

2 Lightly draw one line down the middle of the oval. Draw a second line across the middle for the eyes.

3 Draw another line from side to side for the tip of the nose. This should be halfway between the eye line and the chin.

4 Draw another line between the nose line and the chin. This is where the mouth will go.

5 Use the lines as a guide to sketch in your features. Start with the eyes. Most people's eyes are more than one eye-width apart.

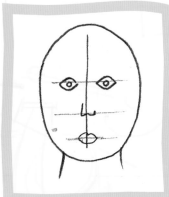

6 Now draw your mouth and the tip of your nose.

7 Add your other features – eyelashes, eyebrows, ears and hair. Usually the bottom of your ears will be level with the tip of your nose.

8 Add some shading using coloured pencils, crayons or chalk.

This self-portrait has been shaded with coloured pencils.

Top tip
When drawing a face, take care to get the eyes, mouth and nose in the right place. Often, people draw the eyes too high up or too far apart.

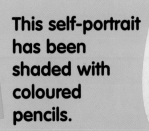

Drawing people

When you draw people, start with simple shapes such as ovals, circles and sausages.

1 Draw an oval for the head at the top of your paper.

2 Add a tube for the neck. Make it almost as wide as the head.

Me and my gran

Draw a picture of yourself with someone special – a brother, sister, grandparent or best friend.

Remember to build up the bodies with circles and ovals. Make the shapes light so you can rub them out later.

Click for Art!

To see chalk drawings by Watteau, go to **www.getty.edu/art/collections/bio/a365-1.html**

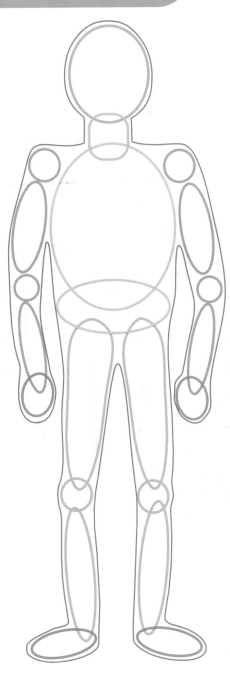

3 Add a large oval for the top part of the body and a smaller oval for the hips.

4 Draw circles for the shoulders, sausage shapes for the upper arms, more circles for the elbows and sausage shapes for the lower parts of the arms.

5 Add the legs in the same way. Make the ovals wider at the top. Add circles for knees, then thinner sausage shapes for the shins.

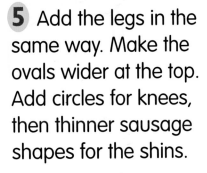

6 Add simple hand and feet shapes, then finish off with the body's **outline**.

Drawing movement

Here's how to make a cardboard figure to help you draw people in different positions.

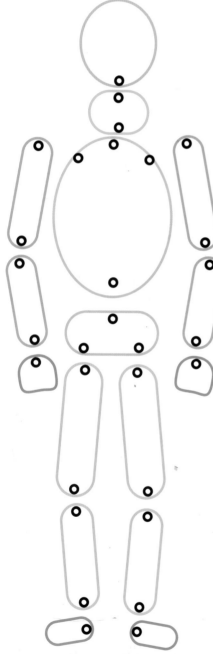

1 Trace the shapes on the left onto tracing paper, then transfer them to white card.

2 Using safety scissors, cut out the cardboard shapes. Push a small hole into each shape with the tip of a ballpoint pen and then fasten the shapes together with split pins.

3 Move the parts of your cardboard body so that it looks as if it is running, jumping or kicking a ball.

4 Use the figure to help you draw body shapes in different positions, or trace around the figure.

Arrange the figure so the body looks as though it is moving naturally

speed lines

Speed lines will help to bring your moving body to life.

If you add straight speed lines, the figure will look as if it is flashing past you.

If you add curved speed lines, the figure will look as if it is twirling or twisting around.

Click for Art!

To see how artists have drawn moving bodies, go to **www.artlex.com** Click on 'Mol-MZ' and scroll down to 'movement' or 'motion'.

Furry animals

You can draw animals in the same way as people, using simple shapes such as circles, ovals and triangles.

Top tip

Real animals are hard to draw because they never keep still! Collect animal pictures in a scrapbook so you can look carefully at the animals' shapes.

1 Draw simple shapes such as circles and ovals first. Make sure the animal's head is smaller than its body.

2 Draw an outline around the shapes. Rub out lines you no longer need.

3 Add details such as the ears, eyes, nose and whiskers.

Drawing fur

To make animals look lifelike, you need to draw the texture of their fur. Here are some different things to try.

Velvety-smooth fur drawn with a soft brown oil pastel

Short, spiky fur drawn with a fine felt-tip pen

Soft, fluffy fur drawn with oil pastel

Shaggy fur drawn with scribbled pencil lines

Click for Art!

For animal drawings by Beatrix Potter, go to **www.peterrabbit.co.uk/beatrixpotter/beatrixpotter1c_a.cfm**
For an outline drawing of a wolf, go to **www.tate.org.uk/collection/** and search on 'Henri Gaudier-Brzeska, A Wolf'.

Here are some other furry animals for you to sketch.

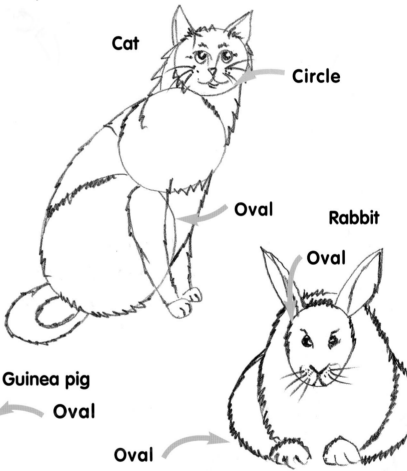

Cat

Circle

Oval

Rabbit

Oval

Oval

4 Add colour and texture for the fur. Look at the yellow box for ways of drawing fur.

Guinea pig

Oval

Circle

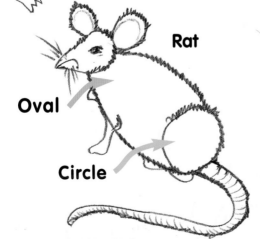

Rat

Oval

Circle

Top tips

Lines and dots can be smudged with your fingertip to make a cat's fur look soft.

Try rubbing out bits of shading with an eraser to make highlights.

15

Fish, reptiles and birds

You can draw fish, reptiles and birds in the same way as cats and dogs, using simple shapes.

Top tip
Birds are the easiest pets to draw – all you need is a circle for the head, an oval body and a long pointed tail.

Budgie

1 Draw a circle and an oval.
2 Add the wing and tail shapes.
3 Add the eye, beak and feet.

Fish face

1 Draw an oval head.
2 Draw two bulging eyes on either side, and a curved mouth.
3 Add the tail and fins.

Snake

1 Start with a simple curved line.
2 Draw the rest of the body.
3 Add the snake's eye, tongue and markings.

Scales and feathers

Scales can be drawn neatly, in rows. Notice how scales often overlap each other. If you like, add some shading.

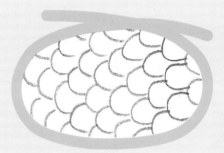

Use long, straight lines to draw large feathers on a bird's wings and tail.

Use short, curved lines to draw short soft feathers on a bird's head and chest.

Lizard

1 Draw two ovals and a tail.
2 Add the legs.
3 Draw patterns on the lizard's body. Don't forget its tongue!

Turtle

1 Draw half an oval for the shell and the head.
2 Add the legs and neck.
3 Draw markings on the shell and legs.

Click for Art!

To see children's drawings of birds and snakes, go to **www.junglephotos.com/** Click on 'Lots more!', then follow the link to 'Children's artwork/St. Mary Magdalene School'.

Cities

City streets are full of exciting shapes. Follow the steps below to make your own city scene.

Top tip

Next time you visit a big city, look carefully at the buildings. What do you notice about the shapes of doors, windows, roofs and chimneys?

1 Lightly sketch the outline of different buildings across the bottom of the paper.

2 Draw taller buildings behind. Use a ruler to keep your lines straight.

City at night

This picture of a city at night has been drawn with bright red, yellow, white and blue crayons on black paper.

Curved sides of buildings make the picture look more exciting

Tiny coloured dashes for lit-up windows

3 Sketch in building details, such as doors and windows. Make the details smaller in the **background**, so some buildings look further away.

4 Go over the outlines of your buildings in wax crayons or pastels. Use a different colour for each building.

5 Colour in the rest of your picture using strong, bright colours. Paint a blue sky behind your city, or cut out your row of buildings and stick it to a sheet of coloured paper.

Click for Art!

To see Robert Delaunay's 'The Red Tower', go to **www.artchive.com/artchive/D/delaunay/red_tower.jpg.html**

Countryside

In the countryside, shapes are rounded and softer than in the city. Follow the steps to draw a scene with different tree shapes and rounded hills.

I Lightly sketch the shape of the trees (look at the green box for help).

You will need:
- A large sheet of cartridge paper
- Coloured chalks, pastels or crayons

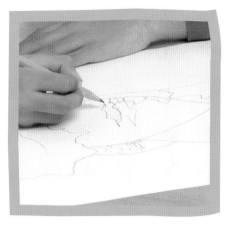

2 Draw the rounded hills. Make them smaller as they get further away.

3 Draw the shapes of smaller trees in the distance.

4 Colour in the drawing with chalks, pastels or crayons.

Drawing trees

1 Lightly sketch the trunk and outline of the tree.

2 Draw the main branches. Make each branch thick near the trunk and thinner at the ends.

3 Use different shades of green for the leaves. Make the top leaves pale and the lower leaves dark, where it is more shady.

Click for Art!

To see a landscape by Monet, go to **www.ibiblio.org/wm/paint/auth/monet/** and click on 'First Impressionist paintings'.

Still life

A still life is a drawing or painting of something that does not move, such as flowers in a vase or a bowl of fruit.

1 Take time arranging the fruit in a bowl or on a tabletop until you are happy with the way it looks.

2 Lightly sketch the outline of the bowl first, then draw the fruit. Start with the pieces at the front of the bowl.

You will need:

- Something to draw, such as a bowl of fruit or a flower
- Coloured pencils, chalks, crayons or pastels

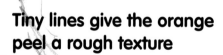

Tiny lines give the orange peel a rough texture

Shading makes the fruit look rounded and three-dimensional

3 Draw the pieces of fruit at the back. Only draw the parts of the fruit that you can see.

4 Go over your outlines in crayon, chalk or pastel.

5 Colour in or shade your picture (see page 6 for ideas).

Top tip

Before you start, look carefully at what you are going to draw. It sounds obvious, but many people who try to draw don't do it!

A colourful still life of flowers in a vase.

Click for Art!

To see still life paintings by Cézanne, go to **www.ibiblio.org/wm/paint/auth/cezanne/sl/**

Glossary

background   area behind the subject of a picture, such as distant hills behind the figure of a horse

cartridge paper   thick, smooth paper for pencil drawings and paintings

features   parts of the face, such as the eyes, nose and mouth, that make each person look different

highlights   bright parts of a picture where there is no shading

outline   the outer shape of an object; usually you draw the outline first, then add the details

shading   adding darker areas to a drawing to make it more realistic

sketchbook   a small, easy-to-carry book for making quick drawings and designs

sugar paper   thick, textured paper often used in scrapbooks

texture   the surface or 'feel' of something: for example, rough, soft, furry, bumpy, smooth or velvety

three-dimensional (3-D)   when something has height, width and depth, instead of just being flat

Index